Awesom

Awesome Kids

A Fun & Fascinating Book of 700 Interesting Facts for Children Aged 8 - 12!

Part of the Awesome Books for Awesome People Series

ANGRY WHIPPET

www.theangrywhippet.com

The Awesome Books For Awesome People Series by The Angry Whippet

Also available:

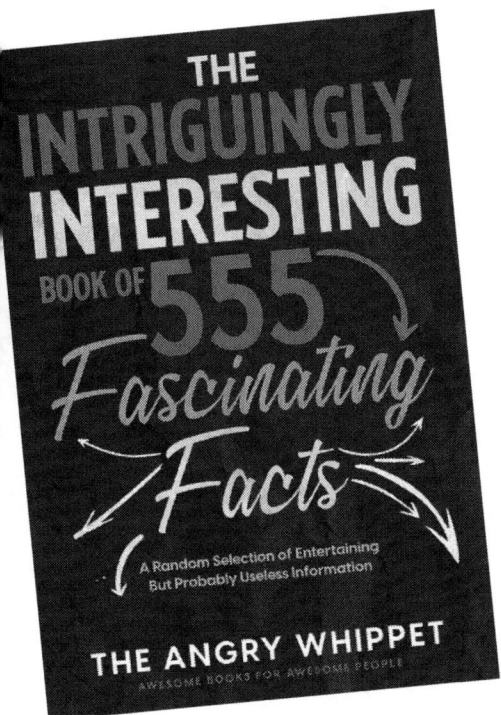

More books on the way, stay tuned!

This book belongs to:

_____

and I am...

Table of Contents

Get ready...

...for some facts!

A Random Selection of Random Facts on a Bunch of Random Things

01 They say that lightning doesn't strike the same place twice, but it does!

02 Your body is made up of 60% water.

03 Your nose can detect a trillion different scents. (That's 1,000,000,000,000!)

04 Dust from the Sahara Desert in Africa can travel as far as Texas in the United States!

05 The Atlantic Ocean is saltier than the Pacific Ocean.

06 Vatican City is the smallest country in the world. It's located inside Rome, which is in Italy.

07 Greenland is the world's largest island.

08 Human teeth are as strong as shark teeth.

09 Banging your head against a wall for one hour will burn 150 calories.

10 You will spend about seventy-nine days of your life brushing your teeth!

11 When dinosaurs existed, there were volcanoes that were erupting on the moon.

12 Your nose gets a little warmer when you tell a lie.

13 Your heart beats around 115,000 times every day.

14 Gorilla's like to burp when they are happy.

15 Some tornadoes are faster than Formula One race cars!

16 The average person laughs about 15 times a day.

17 In a room with 23 people, there's a 50% chance that two people share a birthday.

18 It's impossible to sneeze with your eyes open.

19 There are 2,000 thunderstorms on Earth every minute.

20 The plastic tips of shoelaces are called "aglets."

21 Cats are not able to taste anything that is sweet.

22 Kangaroos can't walk backwards.

23 Wind is silent until it blows against something.

24 There are about 30 million bacteria living on every square inch of the human body!

25 In the Pokemon games, Poliwag & Ditto have the same cry sounds.

26 The flashes of light you see when you rub your eyes are called "phosphenes."

27 The largest pumpkin pie ever baked weighed 2,020 pounds (just over 916 kg.)

28 Strawberries can be red, yellow, green, or white.

29 Bees can sting other bees if they feel threatened or are protecting their territory.

30 Horses and cows can sleep standing up, though they also often sleep lying down.

31 "Odontophobia" is the fear of teeth.

32 It takes about 50 licks to finish just one scoop of ice cream.

33 A chameleon's tongue can be longer than its body.

34 The fastest recorded raindrop was moving at 18 miles per hour.

35 You can't hum a song while holding your nose closed.

36 Male cats have longer tails than female cats.

37 There are more trees on Earth than stars in the Milky Way galaxy.

38 Your fingernails grow faster in warmer weather.

39 The colors of a rainbow always appear in the same order.

40 A prawn's heart is located at the bottom of its head!

41 The United States gets over 1,200 tornadoes a year.

42 12% of people dream in black and white.

43 It is estimated that for every two million lobsters born, one is bright blue. Shiny!

44 The furry bits inside a cat's ears are called "ear furnishings."

45 The sunset on Mars is blue.

46 If you could fold a piece of paper in half 42 times, it would reach the moon.

47 An ostrich's eye is bigger than its brain.

48 Elephants are the only mammals that can't jump.

49 Dolphins only shut half their brain off when sleeping so that they can detect predators.

50 Hawaiian pizza was invented by a Greek man who lived in Canada.

51 A baby puffin is called a "puffling."

52 Dogs can hear 10 times better than humans!

53 A fox uses its tail to communicate with other foxes.

54 People spend about two and half days each year looking for lost objects.

55 Giraffes only have bottom teeth!

56 Pineapples take two years to grow.

57 Venus spins in the opposite direction of other planets.

58 Cows have best friends and they get upset when they are separated.

59 Scotland has over 400 words for "snow."

60 McDonald's once made bubblegum-flavored broccoli.

61 Your nose and ears will grow for your entire life.

62 Some species of snail can have over 20,000 teeth.

63 There are around 6 to 10 million different species of insects.

64 The sun is about 10,000 degrees Fahrenheit, or 5,537 Celsius.

65 Octopuses have three hearts.

66 Sweden has 267,570 islands, the most of any country in the world.

67 You will spend 25 years of your life sleeping!

68 A group of frogs is called an "army."

69 March 14 is Save A Spider Day in the United States.

70 When you blush, the inside of your stomach also turns red.

71 Australia has pink lakes!

72 All apes laugh when they're tickled.

73 Around 11% - 12% of people in the world are left-handed.

74 The average star is between one and ten billion years old.

75 Women's hearts beat faster than men's.

76 Hippopotamus milk is pink!

77 Cows can walk up stairs but not down them.

78 Glass balls can bounce higher than rubber ones.

79 Wrestling is thought to be the world's first sport.

80 The dinosaur with the longest name is "Micropachycephalosaurus."

81 Chimpanzees use tools more than any other animal except humans.

82 There are 336 dimples on a golf ball.

83 Baby rabbits are called "kits!"

84 Butterflies taste with their feet.

85 The front of a giraffe's tongue is dark in color. It's usually purple, blue or black!

86 Birds can sleep with one eye open and one eye shut to watch out for predators.

87 Tarantula spiders can survive two and a half years without food.

88 Slugs have four noses.

89 A tiger's skin has stripes, not just its fur.

90 120 million new red blood cells are being formed in your body every minute.

91 Baby flamingos are born gray, not pink.

92 A group of owls is called a "parliament."

93 A starfish can turn its stomach inside out.

94 Fires spread faster uphill than downhill.

95 Frogs can't swallow with their eyes open.

96 Clouds look white because they are reflecting the sunlight from above them.

97 Porcupines can float.

98 Pigs can't look all the way up at the sky.

99 There are about 40 million donkeys in the world.

100 Australia has the most beaches in the world.

101 The national animal of Scotland is the unicorn.

102 Japan has 23 vending machines per person.

103 Although very rare, snakes can be born with two heads. When it happens, the two heads will fight each other for food.

104 Woodpeckers wrap their tongues around their brain to protect it when pecking.

105 The most leaves ever found on a clover is 56.

106 There is a town called Santa Claus in Indiana, United States.

107 Human bodies contain small traces of gold!

108 If you heat up a magnet, it will lose its magnetism.

109 Every minute of the day, humans shed tens of thousands of skin cells.

110 A hippo's lips are nearly two feet wide.

111 Cockroaches have white blood!

112 A pet hamster can run up to six miles a night on a wheel.

FACTS ABOUT
SPACE

113 Our solar system is in a galaxy called The Milky Way.

114 There are 8 planets in our solar system - Mercury, Venus, Earth, Mars, Jupiter, Saturn, Uranus and Neptune.

115 There are somewhere between 100 and 400 billion stars in our galaxy.

116 It is estimated that there are 2 trillion galaxies in the universe!

117 Our solar system is 4.57 billion years old.

118 It takes 1.3 seconds for light from the Moon to travel to Earth.

119 You can't use a pen in Space because there is no gravity to pull the ink down!

120 Mercury has no atmosphere, which means there is no wind or weather.

121 One day on Mercury is equivalent to 58 days on Earth.

122 The temperature in Space is about -518.81 Fahrenheit, or -270.45 Celsius.

123 Mercury & Venus are the only two planets in our solar system that have no moons.

124 The center of a comet is called a "nucleus."

125 The hottest planet in our solar system is Venus.

126 The tides in the oceans are caused by the gravitational pull of the Moon.

127 The Moon has "moonquakes" that are caused by the gravitational pull of the Earth.

128 One year on Neptune lasts last for 165 Earth years.

129 Mercury is the smallest planet in the Solar System.

130 A year on Mercury is just 88 days long.

131 Mars is the only planet in our solar system that humans might be able to live on.

132 The Sun is 109 times wider than the Earth and 330,000 times as big!

133 The temperature inside the Sun can reach 27,000,000 Fahrenheit, or 15,000,000 Celsius.

134 A light-year is a measurement of how long it takes light to travel in one Earth year.

135 Light travels at 186,282 miles per second, and it would take a human around 37,200 years to travel one light-year.

136 There is a planet 40 light-years away called 55 Cancri e that is thought to be made mostly of diamond.

137 Earth is the only planet in our solar system not named after a Roman god.

138 Mars has the tallest mountain in the solar system. It is called Olympus Mons and is just over 13 miles high.

139 Mars has two small moons. One is called Phobos, and the other Deimos.

140 In the next 20 – 40 million years, Phobos will be torn apart by gravity, creating a ring around Mars that will last up to 100 million years.

141 Comets orbit the Sun the same way as planets do.

142 Space is completely silent.

143 Saturn would float on water because it is made mostly of gas!

144 On Venus, it snows metal and rains acid.

145 We always see the same side of the Moon, no matter where we stand on Earth.

146 Outer space is only 62 miles away.

147 Only 5% of the entire universe can be seen from Earth.

148 There are more stars in space than there are grains of sand in the world.

149 In our solar system there are 4 planets known as gas giants: Jupiter, Saturn, Uranus & Neptune.

150 Venus has the most volcanoes out of all the planets in our solar system.

151 Pluto is smaller than the United States.

152 There are 79 known moons orbiting Jupiter.

153 Jupiter is the fourth brightest object in the solar system.

154 Jupiter has the shortest day of all the planets at just 9 hours and 55 minutes.

155 Neutron stars are the densest and tiniest stars in the universe, have a radius of about 6 miles, and spin 600 times a second.

156 Earth's Moon is the fifth largest moon in the solar system.

157 A year on Saturn lasts for 29 Earth years.

158 The Great Red Spot on Jupiter is a huge storm that has lasted for at least 350 years.

159 Saturn is made mostly of hydrogen.

160 If two pieces of the same type of metal touch in space, they will permanently bond. This is known as "cold welding."

161 The Sun is expanding and will engulf the Earth 5 billion years from now. Yikes!

162 When you look at a star, what you actually see is how it was in the past many light-years ago.

163 Saturn has 83 moons!

164 One year on Uranus is 84 Earth years.

165 Uranus has the coldest temperatures of any planet, dropping down to -371 Fahrenheit, or -224 Celsius.

166 About 1.4 billion years ago, a day on Earth was just 18 hours and 41 minutes long.

167 Shooting stars are bits of space debris that burn up when they enter Earth's atmosphere.

168 Outer space is very cold with a temperature of around -454.75 Fahrenheit, or -270.42 Celsius - the coldest temperature possible!

169 Uranus has two sets of very thin dark colored rings.

170 Neptune is the most distant planet from the Sun.

171 Neptune is one of two "ice giants" in our solar system. The other one is Uranus.

172 Neptune has 14 moons.

173 A rocket needs to travel at 17,600 miles per hour to get into the Earth's orbit.

174 The moon doesn't produce its own light, it actually reflects light from the Sun.

175 The longest time an astronaut has spent in space is 437 days.

176 If you could fly a plane to Pluto, the trip would take more than 800 years.

177 Uranus rotates on its side at a nearly 90 degree angle, the only planet to do so.

178 Earth is hit by an asteroid about the size of a car roughly once a year. Most of it burns up in the atmosphere before it hits land.

179 The sun is made up of around three quarters hydrogen and one quarter helium.

180 Over 90% of the universe is still undiscovered.

181 Much like the Earth revolves around the Sun, the Sun itself revolves around the center of the Milky Way.

182 There are around 500,000 pieces of junk floating around in Space, all left by humans.

183 The first living creatures sent to Space were fruit flies. They were sent up in 1947 and recovered alive.

184 In 1971, an astronaut called Alan Shepard played golf on the Moon!

THE HUMAN BODY

185 Human lungs contain almost 1,500 miles of airways!

186 Your sense of smell is around 10,000 times more sensitive than your sense of taste.

187 The brain uses over a quarter of the oxygen used by the human body.

188 The average person blinks around 8 million times a year.

189 Our eyes are made up of over 2 million working parts.

190 When listening to music, your heartbeat can sync with the rhythm.

191 In one year, your heart will pump enough blood to fill an Olympic size swimming pool.

192 One quarter of your bones are in your feet.

193 There are more than 100,000 miles of blood vessels in your body.

194 Your left kidney is higher up than your right kidney due to the size of the liver.

195 Throughout their lifespan, humans go from having 300 bones to 206 bones.

196 Humans can glow in the dark! However, the glow is too weak for the human eye to detect.

197 Stomach acid can dissolve metal. If it touched your skin, it would burn right through it.

198 The world's most common eye color is brown.

199 Your small intestine is taller than you and measures about 23 feet.

200 Humans are a little taller in the morning than they are at night.

201 The smallest bone in your body is in the inner ear.

202 Babies only blink once or twice a minute.

203 The human body contains more than 600 muscles.

204 The jaw muscle is the strongest muscle in the human body.

205 While awake, your brain produces enough electricity to light a light bulb.

206 Your body carries about four pounds (1.8 kg) of bacteria.

207 Skin is the human body's largest organ.

208 The thigh bone, known as the femur, is the longest bone in the human body.

209 You can't breathe and swallow at the same time!

210 Goose bumps were a way of making our ancestors' hair stand up, to make them appear more threatening to predators.

211 Yuck! Earwax is actually a type of sweat!

212 Your tongue has somewhere between 2,000 – 8,000 taste buds, and each one has up to 100 cells to help you taste your food!

213 The only muscle that never gets tired is the heart.

214 Your body has between 2 and 4 million sweat glands.

215 The scientific name for stomach growls is "borborygmus."

216 The cornea (in the eye) is the only part of the body with no blood supply. It gets its oxygen directly from the air.

217 Your brain won't be fully formed until you are 25 years old.

218 Information travels to your brain at a speed of 268 miles per hour.

219 Your skin contributes to about 15% of your body weight.

220 Bone is a living tissue that constantly renews itself. Your skeleton is completely new every 5 to 10 years.

221 If your eyes were cameras, they'd have about 576 megapixels.

222 The left side of your brain controls the right side of your body, and the right side of your brain controls the left side of your body.

223 50% of your hand strength comes from your little finger.

224 Sometimes the pain from scratching makes your body release a pain-fighting chemical called serotonin, and this can make the itch even itchier!

225 Only 2% of humans have green eyes.

226 A man named Charles Osborne had hiccups for 68 years!

227 80% of your body heat is lost through your head.

228 Every 3 – 4 seconds, around 50,000 cells in your body will die and be replaced by new ones.

229 Your body takes around 12 hours to totally digest food that you've just eaten.

230 Your big toe bears around 40% of your overall body weight.

231 Out of every 200 people, one person will have an extra rib.

232 Less than 4% of the world's population has natural red hair.

233 You use 17 muscles to smile, but use 43 to frown and be miserable.

234 You burn more calories being asleep than you do by watching TV.

235 There are possibly more bacteria in your mouth than there are people in the entire world.

236 When you sneeze, it travels at around 100 miles per hour!

237 The average person spends five years of their life eating.

238 The space between your eyebrows is called the "glabella."

239 Tiny mites that are invisible to the eye are living in your eyelashes.

240 Humans are the only creatures on Earth that produce tears through emotion.

241 Around 1 in every 2,000 babies are born with a tooth.

242 Your nose, along with your brain, can remember around 50,000 different scents.

243 Facial hair is the fastest growing hair on the body (if you have it!)

244 Your left lung is smaller than your right lung to make room for your heart.

245 A large amount of the dust in your home is actually dead skin.

246 An eyelash lives for about 150 days before it falls out.

247 Human teeth are the only part of the body that cannot heal themselves.

248 Your veins have valves that make sure blood only flows in one direction.

249 There are around 67 different species of bacteria living in the average belly button.

250 The soles of your feet contain more sweat glands and nerve endings per inch than any other part of the body.

251 Just like fingerprints, the human tongue has a unique pattern too.

252 There are over 100,000 hairs found on the average scalp.

253 It would take 3,000 years to count the number of nerve cells in the brain.

254 All humans are over 99% identical.

255 Your eyelids have the thinnest amount of skin on your body.

256 An adult human's blood travels around 12,000 miles a day.

Under the Sea

257 Oceans cover nearly 71% of Earth's surface.

258 The five world oceans are the Pacific Ocean, the Atlantic Ocean, the Indian Ocean, the Southern Ocean and the Arctic Ocean.

259 The lowest known point on Earth is called Challenger Deep, and is 35,827 feet (or 10,920 meters) deep.

260 Explorers of the sea are sometimes called "oceanauts."

261 97% of Earth's water is contained in the oceans.

262 The ocean is home to nearly 95% of all life.

263 There's enough gold in the ocean for each of us to have nine pounds of it!

264 There are about one million species of animals living in the ocean.

265 Sound travels 4.3 times faster underwater than it does through the air.

266 Only 5% of the seafloor has been mapped by scientists. We know more about the Moon than we do about our own oceans!

267 The largest ocean animal is the blue whale.

268 A species of shark known as the frilled shark can be pregnant for 3 and a half years.

269 Greenland sharks can live for over 400 years!

270 About 5 trillion pieces of plastic are floating on the world's seas.

271 The planet's longest mountain range is underwater. It's called the Mid-Atlantic Ridge, and is 37,000 miles long.

272 It's very rare, but some starfish can be born square!

273 The Pacific is the largest ocean.

274 Great White sharks have around 300 teeth at any one time, and can lose 20,000 teeth in a lifetime.

275 Sea turtles get rid of salt through their eyes as their kidneys can't process all of it.

276 A type of shrimp called the mantis shrimp can throw a 50 mile per hour punch, the fastest of all the creatures in the world.

277 Octopuses have blue blood.

278 Pygmy seahorses almost never move in their entire lives, and may only ever move around within an area the size of a dinner plate.

279 Dolphins belonging to different groups have different accents.

280 Distances on the ocean are measured in nautical miles, which are about 1.15 times the length of a regular mile.

281 On average, the water in the ocean is 3.5% salt.

282 The Pacific Ocean is the world's deepest ocean, and the Arctic is the shallowest.

283 Tsunamis are huge and devastating waves caused by underwater earthquakes, landslides, or volcanic eruptions.

284 A blue whale's tongue is heavier than an elephant.

285 Crabs have taste buds on their feet.

286 More than 70% of the Earth's oxygen is produced by the ocean.

287 Ninety percent of the Earth's volcanic activity happens in the ocean.

288 It is estimated there are more than 3 million shipwrecks on the ocean floor.

289 There are more historical artifacts under the sea than in all of the world's museums.

290 The Great Barrier Reef in Australia can be seen from the moon.

291 There are more than 400 species of sharks in the ocean.

292 Jellyfish have been around for at least 600 million years.

293 The calls of blue whales are the loudest sound made by any animal on the planet, and can be heard up to 100 miles away.

294 Seahorses are the only animals in which the male, not the female, gives birth and cares for their young.

295 Turtles live on every continent except Antarctica.

296 The pressure at the bottom of the ocean is so great, it would be like a single person trying to hold up 50 airplanes.

ANIMALS, INSECTS & Other Critters

297 There are around 900 million dogs in the world!

298 The regal horned lizard can defend itself by squirting blood out of its eyes.

299 Dogs and cats have unique nose prints, just like human fingerprints.

300 Rats are ticklish, and they laugh when they are tickled.

301 Cats can rotate their ears 180 degrees.

302 Otters hold hands while sleeping so that they don't float away from each other.

303 Hummingbirds are the only known birds that can also fly backwards.

304 African elephants are the largest land animals on Earth.

305 In the wild, some reindeers travel more than 3000 miles in a single year.

306 There are more than 1,400 bat species in the world.

307 There are nearly 10,000 different species of bird.

308 A ladybug can eat more than 5,000 insects in its lifetime!

309 Polar bears are not white, their fur is actually transparent.

310 Koalas can sleep for up to 22 hours a day.

311 One third of our food exists because of bee pollination.

312 Caterpillars have 12 eyes but are almost completely blind.

313 A cockroach can live up to a week without a head.

314 Centipedes never have 100 legs. They usually have between 30 and 380, and it will always be an odd number.

315 Spider silk is actually a liquid. It hardens when it touches the air.

316 You are almost never more than 10 feet away from a spider.

317 Every cricket has its own distinctive song.

318 A group of parrots is known as a "pandemonium."

319 The average worker wasp will only live for 12 – 22 days. The queen can live for up to a year.

320 The fastest land animal on the planet is a cheetah, and can reach speeds of up to 75 miles per hour.

321 Bats are the only mammals that can fly!

322 Dragonflies can see in all directions at the same time.

323 A giraffe has seven bones in its neck – the same as a human!

324 The whale shark produces the biggest eggs in the world, however the babies hatch inside the mother before being born.

325 Cheetahs only need to drink once every three or four days.

326 A bee's wings beat 190 times a second.

327 Mosquitoes are attracted to smelly feet!

328 Grasshoppers existed before dinosaurs.

329 A tiger's roar can be heard as far as two miles away.

330 Giant anteaters can eat over 30,000 insects a day.

331 Starfish have no brain and no blood!

332 Baby elephants are able to stand within 20 minutes of being born.

333 Some chickens lay eggs that are green or blue.

334 Thanks to their special feathers, barn owls are completely silent when they fly.

335 Crows can recognize human faces.

336 Female lions do about 90% of the hunting.

337 Baby elephants suck their trunks for comfort.

338 A flea can jump distances 200 times their body length.

339 A sea creature known as the colossal squid has eyes as big as basketballs.

340 An ostrich's legs are so powerful that their kicks can kill a lion.

341 Polar bears have jet black skin under their fur coats.

342 The smell of a skunk is powerful enough for a human to smell it up to 3.5 miles (5.6 km) away.

343 Rabbits don't have pads on their paws, only fur.

344 Almost two-thirds of the bears in the world live in North America.

345 Mosquitoes are the deadliest creatures on Earth.

346 Snails can sleep for three years at a time.

347 Honey bees have hair on their eyes.

348 Locusts can eat their own weight in food in a day.

349 Baby robins eat 14 feet of earthworms every day!

350 The praying mantis is the only insect that can look behind its shoulders.

351 There are worms in Australia that are over four feet long.

352 A huge bird known as the shoebill stork can swallow a baby crocodile whole.

353 An electric eel can give a shock strong enough to knock out a horse.

354 Cuckoo birds hide their eggs in the nests of other species.

355 Meerkats train their young to hunt scorpions.

356 Wood frogs spend seven months of the year frozen by ice. Their hearts and blood flow stop, and once winter ends they spring back to life!

357 There are more than 50,000 species of spider worldwide.

358 There are around 8.7 million species of creature on Earth. Over 80% of them are undiscovered.

359 Only female mosquitoes bite.

360 Puffins use twigs to scratch their bodies.

361 Sloths can take up to a month to completely digest a single leaf.

362 Some pigs in China are the size of bears.

363 Zebra stripes act as a natural bug repellent.

364 A group of ferrets is called a "business."

365 Alligators can grow for more than 30 years.

366 Cows can produce more milk when listening to slow music.

367 Greyhounds are the world's fastest dogs, and can reach speeds of up to 45 miles per hour.

368 Reindeer's eyes turn blue in winter to help them see at lower light levels.

A Short Section on History

369 Ketchup was sold in the 1830s as a cure for an upset stomach.

370 Abraham Lincoln was a great wrestler, and only lost one out of 300 contests.

371 From 1912 to 1948, the Olympic Games held competitions in the fine arts. Medals were given for literature, architecture, sculpting, painting, and music.

372 Roman emperor Augustus Caesar was the wealthiest man to ever live in history.

373 There were female Gladiators in Ancient Rome. A female gladiator was called a Gladiatrix.

374 Instead of saying "cheese" when having a photo taken, people used to say "prunes!"

375 A horse was once made a senator in Ancient Rome.

376 The Vikings explored America 500 years before Christopher Columbus did.

377 The Eiffel Tower in France was originally meant to be in Barcelona, Spain.

378 The Ancient Egyptians invented toothpaste. It was made of rock salt, pepper, mint, and dried flowers.

379 There are around 5,000 years of recorded history.

380 In 18th century England, pineapples were only owned by rich people. They carried them around to show how wealthy they were.

381 100 million years ago, the Sahara Desert was inhabited by galloping crocodiles.

382 In Britain and Ireland, people known as "knocker-uppers" used to wake people up for work by tapping on their windows early in the morning.

383 The last queen of Egypt, Cleopatra, wasn't born in Egypt, she was Greek.

384 Turkeys were once worshiped as gods by the Mayans, an ancient civilization from Central America.

385 The United States of America bought Alaska from the Russians in 1867.

386 History is generally divided into 4 time periods: Prehistory, Ancient History, Post-Ancient History, and Modern History.

387 The construction of The Great Wall of China started in 680 BC, and wasn't finished until 1681 AD.

388 The ninjas of ancient Japan were called "shinobi."

389 In the thirteenth century, Pope Gregory IX declared a war on cats.

390 Macedonian King Alexander the Great conquered over 2 million square miles of the Earth's surface by the time he was 30.

391 In medieval England, the word "ask" was pronounced "ax."

392 Ancient Egyptians used slabs of stone as pillows.

SCIENCE STUFF

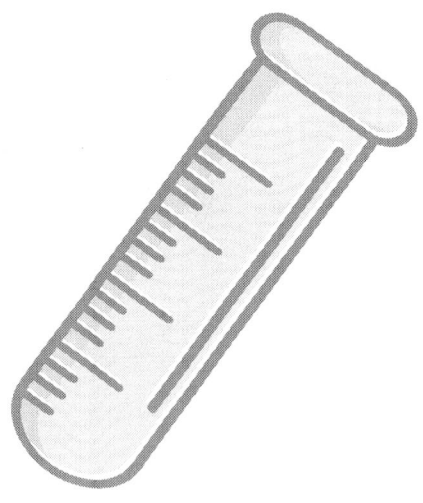

393 Astronomy, the study of everything outside of our planet, is the oldest science.

394 Hot water freezes quicker than cold water.

395 Tooth enamel is stronger than bones.

396 Although oxygen gas is colorless, the liquid and solid forms of oxygen are blue.

397 The only letter that doesn't appear on the periodic table is "J."

398 Bee stings are acidic while wasp stings are alkaline.

399 If you exposed a glass of water to space, it would boil rather than freeze.

400 Air becomes liquid at -321 Fahrenheit (-190 Celsius.)

401 The human body contains enough carbon to produce graphite for about 9,000 pencils.

402 Helium is the only chemical element that can't be solidified.

403 Copper is the only metal that is naturally antibacterial.

404 If you slowly pour a handful of salt into a completely full glass of water, it will not overflow.

405 DNA is a flame retardant.

406 Helium and hydrogen account for 98% of all matter.

407 The colors in fireworks are made possible by using different salts with different metals.

408 The density of ice is 10% lower than that of water, which is why ice floats on water.

409 The study of how heat relates to other forms of energy is called "thermodynamics."

410 The word "physics" comes from the Greek word "physike," which means "science of nature."

411 According to Albert Einstein, the farther an object is from the Earth's surface, the faster time passes.

412 Energy cannot be created or destroyed, but it can change forms.

413 Heat cannot travel to an area that is warmer than its current one.

414 The pain we feel from the venom of wasp and bee stings is due to the enzymes in the venom breaking down our cells.

415 The faster you travel, the slower time goes for you.

416 There are invisible kinds of light, like X-rays, radio waves and ultraviolet.

417 Transparent objects are visible only because they reflect light.

418 Wind has shadows that can't be seen by the naked eye.

419 You need temperatures of over 1,832 Fahrenheit (1,000 Celsius) to burn a diamond.

420 The ozone layer handles the absorption of most of the ultraviolet radiation from the sun.

421 The heaviest element by density is osmium, a shiny silver metal that resists corrosion.

422 Diamonds are the hardest material found on Earth.

423 Frogs are able to absorb moisture from their skin, meaning they do not need to drink water.

424 Lightning can reach temperatures over 54,000 Fahrenheit (30,000 Celsius.)

425 Different flame colors indicate different degrees of heat.

426 Balloons will only float when they are filled with gasses that are lighter than air, such as helium.

427 "Dry ice" is the term used for frozen carbon dioxide.

428 Lobster blood is colorless until exposed to oxygen.

429 Water is known as "dihydrogen monoxide" in chemical terms.

430 Copper and gold are the only non-silvery types of metals.

431 Hydrofluoric acid is so corrosive that it can dissolve glass.

432 Astatine is a rare element that occurs naturally in the crust of the Earth. There are less than 28 grams of astatine on Earth at any given time.

433 The Earth spins at 1,000 miles per hour and travels through space at 67,000 miles per hour.

434 10% of all human beings ever born are alive at this very moment.

435 The largest ever hailstone weighed over 2.2 pounds (1kg) and fell in Bangladesh in 1986.

436 The adult human body has an average of 7,000 white blood cells. These cells are used by the body to fight infections.

437 Space has a smell. It's been described as a blend between grilled meat, hot metal and fuel.

438 The Great Barrier Reef in Australia is the largest living structure on Earth. It's 1,429 miles long!

439 About 1% of our genes come from plants, fungi, and many other microorganisms.

440 There are 3 major branches of biology – botany (plants), zoology (animals), and microbiology (living organisms too small to see.)

441 One inch of rain can equal up to 10 inches of snow, depending on the temperature.

442 You cannot taste anything without saliva.

443 Chalk is made up of trillions of microscopic skeleton fossils of plankton – tiny organisms found in water.

444 Fish scales are commonly used as an ingredient to make lipstick.

445 Stale eggs will float in water. Fresh eggs will sink.

446 Bromine and mercury are the only elements that can stay liquid at room temperature.

447 Many radioactive elements glow in the dark.

448 Your tooth enamel is the hardest chemical substance in your body.

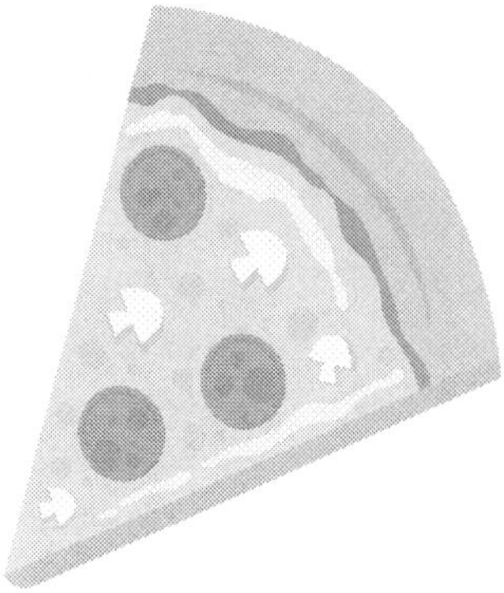

FOOD GLORIOUS FOOD

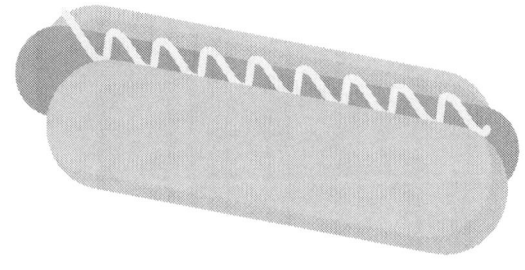

449 Applesauce was the first food eaten in space.

450 Pistachios aren't nuts, they are actually fruits!

451 Most wasabi is just horseradish that's dyed green.

452 Cashews are the fruit of cashew apples.

453 "Arachibutyrophobia" is the fear of getting peanut butter stuck to the roof of your mouth.

454 Pound cake is called pound cake because there was a pound of every ingredient in the original recipe.

455 Most carrots are orange, but they can also be purple and yellow.

456 Cucumbers are mostly water.

457 One fast-food burger can have meat from 100 different cows.

458 American cheese was invented in Switzerland.

459 Cheese is the most stolen food in the world. Around 4% of all cheese made around the globe is stolen!

460 One in four hazelnuts ends up in a jar of Nutella.

461 McDonald's sells around 2.5 billion hamburgers every year.

462 Peanuts have an oil that can be used as an ingredient when making dynamite.

463 In ancient Egyptian days, radishes, onions, and garlic were given to workers as wages.

464 Broccoli contains more protein per calorie than steak.

465 Potatoes were the first food planted in space.

466 Figs aren't fruit, they're actually flowers.

467 The filling inside Kit Kats is made from broken Kit Kat bars that get rejected after being made.

468 Almonds are not nuts. They are the seeds of an almond fruit.

469 Cotton candy, also known as candy floss, was created by a dentist.

470 There are fruit salad trees that grow up to six different types of fruit.

471 Lemons float – but limes sink.

472 A single spaghetti noodle is called a "spaghetto."

473 A fear of cooking is known as "mageirocophobia."

474 French fries aren't from France, they were developed in Belgium.

475 "Pomology" is the study of fruit, specifically the science of growing fruit and nuts.

476 Margherita pizza was created in 1889, and was named after the Queen of Italy at the time – Queen Margherita!

477 Cauliflower can be white, green, purple and orange.

478 Eating kiwi helps your body process protein, which is important for muscle growth.

479 Eggplants aren't vegetables, they're fruits!

480 There are more than 3,000 varieties of pears in the world, and America produces 84% of them.

481 The heaviest tomato ever grown in the world weighed 8.61 pounds (3.9 kg.)

482 Ripe cranberries will bounce.

483 Bird saliva is an ingredient used in a soup in China called... Bird's nest soup!

484 Human DNA is 60% the same as bananas.

485 Tonic water glows in the dark under certain lights.

486 Most of us use refrigerators to keep our food cold. Eskimos use them to stop their food from freezing!

487 Australians eat the most meat out of any country.

488 There are over 600 different types of pasta shapes produced worldwide.

489 "Alliumphobia" is the fear of garlic.

490 There are more than 10,000 different varieties of tomatoes.

491 Termites and ants are roasted and eaten like popcorn in South Africa.

492 There are over 7,000 different varieties of apples in the world.

493 One cluster of bananas is called a "hand."

494 Turning a pineapple upside-down will make it ripen faster.

495 People from Britain eat over 300 million portions of fish and chips each year.

496 The popsicle was invented by an 11-year-old called Frank Epperson.

497 The Aztecs used chocolate as currency.

498 Avocados won't ripen on the tree.

499 One ostrich egg is the equivalent of 24 chicken eggs.

500 One pound of dried saffron requires 75,000 saffron flowers.

501 Farm-raised salmon is naturally white and then dyed pink.

502 Potatoes can absorb and reflect Wi-Fi signals.

503 Honey will never ever go bad.

504 Rhubarb grows so fast that you can actually hear it creaking and popping as it gets bigger.

Our Planet

505 The Earth is not perfectly round. It is flattened at the North and South poles.

506 Russia is the biggest country in the world.

507 Mexico City was built on a lake in 1325, and is currently sinking by about 3.2 feet per year.

508 Earth is about 4.54 billion years old.

509 There are currently seven continents in our world. They are Asia, Africa, North America, South America, Antarctica, Europe, and Australia.

510 Asia is the largest continent, containing countries like China and India.

511 The driest place on Earth, the Atacama Desert, is right next to the world's biggest body of water – the Pacific Ocean.

512 The United States has the most states in the world.

513 Australia is the world's smallest continent.

514 All the continents on Earth were once one giant continent called Pangea.

515 The tallest mountain in the world is called Mauna Kea, and is 33,500 feet tall (including the bit that's under the ocean!)

516 Iceland is growing 2 inches each year as the plates underneath grow wider apart.

517 The Sargasso Sea is found in the Atlantic Ocean, and is the only sea in the world that doesn't have any coasts.

518 Kentucky, in the United States, has more caves than any other place on Earth.

519 Deserts aren't always hot. The largest desert in the world is the Antarctic Polar Desert.

520 The world's largest hot desert is the Sahara Desert in Africa.

521 Europe is the second smallest continent, but has the third largest population.

522 The Amazon is Earth's biggest rainforest, and is located in South America.

523 Greenland is the world's largest island.

524 The oldest tree in the world, the bristlecone pine, is almost 5,000 years old.

525 The longest river in the world is the River Nile, which is found in Africa. It is just over 4,250 miles long.

526 It snows more in Japan than anywhere else in the world.

527 It would take you around 18 months to walk all the way along The Great Wall of China.

528 The Great Wall of China is so great, it can be seen from space!

529 There are 195 countries in the world.

530 Earth is the only planet in the solar system that has liquid water on its surface.

531 The Earth was once covered with giant mushrooms that could grow up to 24 feet tall.

532 Without the Moon's gravitational pull slowing down the Earth's spinning, a day would only be six hours long.

533 There are between 10 to 20 volcanoes erupting somewhere on Earth every day.

534 The atmosphere of Earth is divided into six layers – the troposphere, stratosphere, mesosphere, thermosphere, exosphere, and ionosphere.

535 700 million years ago, the entire Earth was covered in ice.

536 11% of the Earth's surface is used to grow food.

537 The Amazon Rainforest supplies 20% of the world's oxygen.

538 It takes 90 days for one drop of water to travel the Mississippi River.

539 Canada is the country with the longest coastline on Earth at 125,000 miles.

540 Coffee originated in Ethiopia.

541 Continents shift at about the same rate as your fingernails grow.

542 90% of Earth's population lives in the Northern Hemisphere (the "top" half of the world.)

543 California has more people than all of Canada.

544 Australia is wider than the moon.

545 The windiest place on Earth is Chicago, United States.

546 In the Philippines, there's an island that's within a lake, on an island that's within a lake, on an island.

547 Russia has more surface area than Pluto.

548 Earth is the only planet in our solar system to have water in all three of its forms - liquid, solid and gas.

549 The Greek name for Earth was Gaia, meaning "Mother Earth."

550 The Earth's core is hotter than the surface of the Sun.

551 Africa is the only continent situated in all four hemispheres - the western, the eastern, the northern and the southern.

552 There is not a single river in Saudi Arabia.

553 The Earth has lost 40% of its wildlife in the past 40 years.

554 The biggest pyramid in the world is not in Egypt, but in Mexico. It is called The Great Pyramid of Cholula.

555 The capital of Turkey, Istanbul, is on two different continents. 65% of it is in Europe, and the other 35% is in Asia.

556 Iceland is the only country with no mosquitoes.

557 The first city to ever have 1 million people living in it was Rome in 133 BC.

558 The village with the longest name in the world is in Wales, United Kingdom. It's called Llanfairpwllgwyngyllgogerychwyrndro-bwllllantysiliogogogoch.

559 The name "Earth" is at least 1,000 years old.

560 All the people in the world could fit in the state of Texas, USA.

TECHNOLOGY
FACTS

561 On average, people read 10% slower from a screen than from paper.

562 When the first VCR (Video Camera Recorder) was made in 1956, it was the size of a piano.

563 There are more than 5.1 billion active users on the internet.

564 Asia accounts for more than 50% of total internet traffic.

565 The first ever computer mouse was carved out of wood and had just one button.

566 The original Xbox had sound snippets of real space missions on the home screen.

567 The first ever mechanical alarm clock, invented in 1787, could only ring at one time – 4am!

568 The barcode was invented in 1952, but wasn't used until 1974.

569 Cuba is the only Caribbean country that has a railway.

570 Nintendo didn't start as a video games company – they originally manufactured playing cards.

571 Amazon wasn't always called Amazon, it was originally called "Cadabra."

572 97% of people type words into Google to see if they spelled them right.

573 Motorola produced the first portable mobile phone.

574 Japan has the fastest internet speed of 319 terabits per second.

575 Nokia's first product was toilet paper.

576 For every 12 million spam emails, only one gets a reply.

577 Google receives more than 99,000 searches every second.

578 There are 4,000 luxury cars at the bottom of the Atlantic Ocean after a cargo ship caught fire and sank.

579 Around 8 billion gadgets connect to the internet every day.

580 Ancient Greece used rail transport as early as the 6th century BC.

581 The first computer virus was named "Creeper."

582 Banks and other corporate giants hire white hats or "good hackers" to help fix security issues and prevent system infiltration.

583 350,000 tweets are sent every minute.

584 92% of all money is stored digitally.

585 The fear of a new technology is called "technophobia."

586 The most common computer password is "123456."

587 The first computer made had a weight of over 27 tons.

588 The QWERTY keyboard was created to let people type more quickly.

589 Around 500,000 new computer viruses are discovered every day.

590 The first 1-gigabyte hard drive weighed as much as a refrigerator.

591 Artificial intelligence may one day allow computers to understand what dogs are thinking.

592 The first ever website went live in 1991.

593 The first text message was sent in 1992, and it said "Merry Christmas!"

594 "Phantom Vibration Syndrome" is the name for when someone thinks their phone is vibrating, but it isn't.

595 The original name of Microsoft Windows was "Interface Manager."

596 Microsoft, Google, Apple and Amazon are businesses that were all started in garages.

597 More than 1.5 billion websites can be found on the World Wide Web today.

598 Minecraft is the best-selling video game of all time.

599 There are over 1 billion active iPhones in the world.

600 YouTube Has 2 billion monthly logged-in users.

FACTS ABOUT COUNTRIES

601 More Armenians live abroad than in Armenia.

602 Croatia is the home of a very popular dog breed – the Dalmatian!

603 Costa Rica doesn't have an army.

604 Cyprus has around 20 rare species of orchid.

605 All men in South Korea are required to serve in the military for 18 months between the ages of 18 and 28.

606 Ecuador is the closest country to Space.

607 Only 60.7% of people in Haiti above the age of 15 can read and write.

608 Singapore has the world's highest percentage of millionaires.

609 Brazil is the largest country in South America.

610 Portugal claimed the land of Brazil in the year 1500. Independence was declared in 1822.

611 The most popular sport in India is cricket.

612 China has the world's largest population – 1.426 billion.

613 French is the second most studied language in the world after English.

614 Besides Vatican City, Italy has another very small country located inside it – it is called "San Marino."

615 Most of the world's tornadoes occur in the Midwest region of the US known as Tornado Alley.

616 It is estimated the humans have lived in Australia for around 45,000 years.

617 The Japanese name for Japan is "Nihon" or "Nippon" which means "sun origin."

618 The official language of Egypt is Arabic, but other languages such as English and French are also understood by many.

619 It is believed that modern humans first arrived in Spain around 32,000 years ago.

620 There are over 1,000 kinds of sausages in Germany.

621 Mexico's real name is the United States of Mexico.

622 South Africa has three capital cities – Pretoria, Cape Town and Bloemfontein.

623 80% of Greece is made up of mountains.

624 The United Kingdom is made up of four countries – England, Scotland, Wales and Northern Ireland.

625 Canadians eat more donuts than any other country in the world.

626 New Zealand has the clearest lake in the world. Nelson's Blue Lake is so clear, you can see all the way down to 262 feet deep.

627 The Netherlands is also known as Holland.

628 Kenya is home to lions, elephants, buffalo and rhinos.

629 Jamaica has 8 native snake species, but none of them are venomous.

630 Turkey is the world's leading hazelnut producer.

631 During the summer in some parts of Norway, the sun never sets.

632 Thailand was previously known as Siam.

633 Halloween was invented in Ireland.

634 The capital of Argentina, Buenos Aires, translates to "good airs" or "fair winds."

635 The world's largest castle, The Castle of Teutonic Order in Malbork, is located in Poland.

636 There are no McDonald's restaurants in Iceland.

637 The national dish of Peru is called Cuy. It is a roasted guinea pig served whole!

638 Christmas was banned in Cuba in 1969. The ban lasted for 30 years.

639 The highest volcano on Earth is in Chile, and is called Ojos del Salado.

640 63% of Sweden is forest.

641 The world's oldest bookstore is in Lisbon, Portugal.

642 Colombia has 18 public holidays each year.

643 The world's biggest flower, the Rafflesia arnoldii, lives in Indonesia.

644 There is no Danish word for "please."

645 Fiji is made up of around 333 islands, and over 220 of them are uninhabited.

646 Madagascar is the world's fourth largest island.

647 There are more banks in Switzerland than there are dentists.

648 Austria is home to Europe's tallest waterfalls – the Krimml Waterfalls. They reach a height of 1,247 feet.

649 The movie industry in Nigeria is known as "Nollywood."

650 Finland is ranked number 1 as the happiest country in the world.

651 There is no Belgian language. People in Belgium speak either Dutch, French or German.

652 Venezuela is home to the world's largest rodent – the Capybara.

653 In Hungary, people can only name children using a name on a pre-approved list by the government. If you want to use a different name, you have to ask.

654 The Czech Republic has the most castles of any country in Europe.

655 Malaysia has a 130 million year old rainforest called Taman Negara. It's twice as old as the Amazon.

656 The national flower of Bangladesh is a white-flowered water lily called Sada Shapla.

A LITTLE BIT OF SPORT

657 There are over 8,000 different sports in the world.

658 A badminton shuttlecock weighs around 0.17 oz (5 g.)

659 Tennis racket strings were traditionally made from the intestines of goats, cows, or sheep.

660 A microwaved baseball will fly further than a frozen baseball, as warmer baseballs weigh less.

661 The longest ever tennis match was played at Wimbledon, UK. It was played over three days and lasted 11 hours and 5 minutes.

662 The chances of a professional golfer making a hole-in-one are 2,500 to 1.

663 Contrary to popular belief, the English invented the word "soccer." They only started calling it football when Americans started using the word soccer as well.

664 The first Olympic Games were held in 776 BC in Olympia, Ancient Greece.

665 Table tennis balls can travel off the paddle at a speed of 105.6 miles per hour.

666 The world record speed for skiing is 158.4 miles per hour.

667 Kite flying is a professional sport.

668 Formula One cars generate so much downforce, they could drive upside down on the roof of a tunnel at a speed of 140 miles per hour.

669 Rugby balls were first made from pig's bladders.

670 Left-handed people are better at particular sports, mainly those that involve spatial judgment and quick reactions.

671 Olympic gold medals are made mostly of silver. They haven't been made of pure gold since 1912.

672 Until 1850, golf balls were made from leather and stuffed with feathers.

673 Volleyball was invented in Massachusetts, USA, in 1985.

674 The grass at Wimbledon tennis courts used to be around 2 inches long, until an English player was bitten by a snake in 1949. Now, it's 0.31 inches long.

675 Bowling was invented around 3200 BC in Egypt.

676 The world record for the most consecutive push-ups is 10,507.

677 The longest boxing match in history lasted 110 rounds and went on for over seven hours.

678 The most people to ever stand on one surfboard is 66.

679 There have been three Olympic Games held in countries that no longer exist – West Germany, USSR and Yugoslavia.

680 Major League Baseball teams use about 850,000 balls per season.

A FEW MORE
RANDOMS

681 The oldest currency in the world is the British pound.

682 The only fears we have at birth are the fear of falling and the fear of loud noises.

683 A shape with 26 sides is known as a "rhombicuboctahedron."

684 There are over 6,000 species of grass.

685 The queens in ant colonies can live for around 5 – 30 years.

686 Kangaroos never stop growing.

687 The Hogwarts Express from the Harry Potter movies is a real train in Scotland.

688 Putting sugar on a cut will make it heal faster.

689 A bolt of lightning contains enough energy to toast 100,000 slices of bread.

690 No two snowflakes are ever the same.

691 Crocodiles are one of the oldest living species, having survived for more than 200 million years.

692 The cracking sound your joints make is the sound of gasses being released.

693 A duel between three people is called a "truel."

694 Most toilet paper sold for home use in France is pink!

695 There's a sport called "squirrel fishing," in which participants try to catch squirrels and lift them into the air by using a nut on a fishing pole.

696 People don't sneeze in their sleep due to their brain shutting down the reflex.

697 Animals that lay eggs don't have belly buttons.

698 Camels have three eyelids.

699 The Hawaiian alphabet only has 12 letters.

700 Honeybees navigate using the sun as their compass.

BONUS FACT!
701

YOU'RE

AWESOME!

I hope you learned a few things!

If this book brought a little joy, then please
consider leaving a review!

Made in the USA
Monee, IL
31 October 2022

16862669R00063